T0128434

Come and Rest

Come and Rest

Invitations for Your Soul to Flourish

LINNEA BERGSTROM

WESTBOW
PRESS®
A DIVISION OF THOMAS NELSON
& ZONDERVAN

WestBow Press books may be ordered through booksellers or by contacting:

WestBow Press
A Division of Thomas Nelson & Zondervan
1663 Liberty Drive
Bloomington, IN 47403
www.westbowpress.com
1 (866) 928-1240

ISBN: 978-1-9736-5659-3 (sc)
ISBN: 978-1-9736-5658-6 (hc)
ISBN: 978-1-9736-5660-9 (e)

Library of Congress Control Number: 2019902798

Print information available on the last page.

WestBow Press rev. date: 3/15/2019

For Sam, Soren, and Eva.

May you always stay rooted in Christ.

Preface

At the age of thirty, in the midst of raising a baby and a toddler, I found myself hungry for purpose and thirsty for more in my life. Chase your dreams; be who you are called to be; dream big; do it scared; you were made for more. I hungrily consumed these beautiful and inspiring messages until I realized that for me, they had become dangerous. They were feeding an increasingly deep discontent.

I would lift my head from the last page of the book just to look around and notice that my life was still the same. My husband was still working sixty-plus hours a week; my toddler still wanted me to make him lunch; my baby's diapers still needed to be changed, and our bank account was still the same number. I would share my newfound dreams and discoveries with my husband. He would hear me out, let me talk, and, with love and grace, he would hit me with reality. We can't afford that. You'd have to do it alone; my job won't allow for that. Who is going to watch the kids?

I would pick up a new book, looking for a new approach and inspiration to live out my dreams. I was trying to be who God made me to be. After all, I was made for more, right? More than staying at home all day up to my eyeballs in laundry and crumbs. And the cycle would start again. Read. Feel empowered. Share dreams. Get shot down. Search for another book. Repeat. A deep discontentment began to set in, and my husband began tuning me out. Another dream. Another time he had to tell me no.

I found myself bitter. Bitter with the beautiful life I was living. Bitter that I couldn't be more. Bitter that my husband's job required him to work weekends. Bitter because I couldn't just do what I wanted to do. I had become blind to all that was good because I was so focused on what I couldn't have or what I thought I should have.

I was tired, overwhelmed, and confused. I turned to God, and my prayer went something like this:

Dear God,

I'm tired. Physically. Emotionally. Spiritually. Mentally. I feel overwhelmed. It seems as though everything is a priority, and there are a lot of *everythings*. Each day feels like there are weights on my feet. I'm trying to get done the things that need to be done and care for the people I need to care for. But it seems like such effort to do the simplest of tasks. It is all compounding. I can't get ahead and stay ahead.

I want to flourish. That sounds beautiful and enticing. I'd want to be around someone who is flourishing. I don't even want to be around me right now. I am critical and controlling. I snap at my kids often and am easily annoyed by my husband. I feel uninspired and joyless. If anything, I feel like a dry and withered leaf. Who wants to be around that? But to flourish! That would be wonderful. I want to love what I have and get rid of the rest. I imagine the feeling of lightness. I want to feel like I'm just floating through my day, my feet never touching the ground.

Maybe I need a change of scenery—literally and figuratively. But would that even help? I don't want to live like this anymore. I want to change. I need a change. But what? I am at a loss. I lay this all before You, Lord. Raw, unfiltered, and openhanded. I'm responsible. I've made the choices in my life, and look where they have gotten me. I need my life to be in Your hands. It's time I surrender. I'm scared. But I don't know what else to do. You, God, have to take care of me, right? You won't let me fall, will You? You love me, right? Jesus loves me, this I know, for the Bible tells me so?

I thought of Erin Loechner's words from her book *Chasing Slow*:

I also wonder if God has given us a few things—an aging parent, some mouths to feed, a recent job loss—and we have given ourselves many more things—the Target credit card bill, a yard to mow, a bigger house with an extra bedroom for guests, three dinner parties to host, and the inability to say no to serving the animal crackers in Sunday school twice this month. Between God's giving and our own giving, there is excess ... and suddenly, we've tipped the scale. We're stressed. We pray for deliverance, for peace, for our joy to return. We call this a test. Can we handle this? Can we handle the busy? Can we handle a quicker pace, a heftier load? Perhaps we were never intended to.

The morning was gorgeous. The sun shone over the fruit trees and through the kitchen window. It does this for only a few minutes each day in September. I love this. The house was quiet. I stood at the window, coffee in hand, looking out over our tiny orchard.

"*Lord,*" I said, "*I lay it all before You. I want to flourish. This is all out in the open now. It feels refreshing to be so honest with You, God. So often I feel like I have to be buttoned up before I approach You in prayer, as though I want You to see that I know the right words to say or the right way to ask You for things. Am I doing this right? I want to learn how to pray, if there is such a thing.*"

I felt the sunrise bathe my face and knew that its light over the fruit trees had drawn me into God's presence. And then into the quiet of my mind came these words:

Linnea, if you want to flourish, you must be pruned first. I want you to study the fruit trees.

And that is how God responded. He told me to study the fruit trees. So I studied the fruit trees. I studied the actual ones we own and studied the ones written about throughout scripture. It wasn't until God called me to start cutting things back in my life (pruning) that I realized what a negative impact I had allowed these books and messages to have on my life. He was telling me to look at life through the lens of less, not more. It was then that beautiful things began to happen.

This book is a response to all I learned (and am still learning) when I studied the fruit trees and when I began cutting back branches that weren't producing fruit. When I cut back even the good branches to keep myself healthy, and when I learned about seasons, roots, soil, fruit, and the harvest. When God shifted my focus from trying to build my life to undoing it, I began to flourish. And those are the themes you will see woven throughout this book.

You get to take what you read each day and make it your own. Take time to carve out a few extra moments to sit with it and allow the ideas to soak into your mind and heart. You will find journal lines for writing out answers to the invitations and your thoughts on the reading. My words are hopefully a new way for you to see scripture and a way for you to carry the Word with you.

I want to always give God the glory. Nothing beautiful in this life is done because of our own doing and power. Transformation, wisdom, healing, ah-ha moments, grace, forgiveness, kindness—these are all because of the grace-full power of God. When we open ourselves up to all God has for us and allow Him to move in our lives, gratitude and worship will grow out of transformation.

Each day is a new invitation—an invitation to

be still and know that He is God, an invitation to stop and check the direction we are headed, and an invitation to surrender to His love. Whether you are dreaming big or scaling back, these are invitations to enter into the journey of seeing all that God might have for you as you slow down, cut back, and make room for more of Him.

Rest

Are you tired? Worn out? Burned out on religion? Come to me. Get away with me and you'll recover your life. I'll show you how to take a real rest. Walk with me and work with me—watch how I do it. Learn the unforced rhythms of grace. I won't lay anything heavy or ill-fitting on you. Keep company with me and you'll learn to live freely and lightly. (Matthew 11:28–30 Message)

R ead the verses again. Take time to really read them. Rest in the words from Jesus. He will not lay anything heavy or ill-fitting on you. You can live free and light in Christ. Rest. This is our invitation from Christ. It is our invitation to come and rest.

Rest does not have to mean an actual physical break from living life. It does not have to mean that you put your feet up, drink tea, and listen to music for hours on end. It does not have to mean you need to get away for a weekend or vacation for a week. Those things are good and helpful for many and are a form of rest. But if we don't rest our minds and our souls, the vacation taken for physical rest will only carry us so far. There comes a point where we need to take a holy pause. We need to lift our heads from our lives and refocus our attention.

Rest is written about all throughout scripture, starting with creation. God rested after He created. He told the Israelites to let their land rest in the seventh year. He told His people to take one day a week to rest. While rest is physical, it is also mental—a time to refocus, a time to check in, and a time just to be.

Rest can be giving yourself permission to let go of the unrealistic expectations you've put on your own life. Rest can be saying no. Rest can be leaning into your gifting and making more time to do what makes you come alive. Rest can be being okay with the only five minutes of quiet you have in the day. Rest can be had while you are moving through your day. Rest can be a mind-set shift from the chasing to the accepting.

INVITATION

Are there areas of your life that you wish you could pause or slow down? What steps can you begin taking to do just that?

How can you rest today?

What is heavy and ill-fitting that you can hand over to God? Give that to Him today.

Be Still

*I*n a world that is so fast paced, it can be hard to just be still. We want so badly to move from one thing to the next. Maybe this is so we don't have time to feel what is really going on. Maybe we get anxious if we are not producing. Maybe we don't know what to do with stillness. I already see it in my kids. They want everything right now, right away, in an instant. And I can't blame them. Everything they have ever known is instant. Dinner happens in less than ten minutes; we fast-forward through commercials, and toys are delivered at the doorstep.

And then we get frustrated that we can't hear God. We don't see Him work. Where are His miracles? Doesn't He care? But what if we weren't created to go at this speed? What if God just moves more slowly than we want him to? Are we subscribing to an instant God, expecting Him to show up at our doorstep in two days or less, and then when He doesn't, we call wondering where He is and why He isn't performing?

There is a beautiful reminder for us in Psalm 46: "Be still, and know that I am God; I will be exalted among the nations, I will be exalted in the earth." Does that verse make you breathe a sigh of relief as well? God is giving us permission to slow down and to be still. And when we do, He will be exalted. His timing is good and perfect. When we are still, we can see Him working and moving, and we learn to trust.

It can be hard though, can't it? Hard to slow down, hard to put the brakes on, and hard to trust. It's a new rhythm we must put in place for ourselves. A rhythm of teaching our soul to be still. With each step toward this new rhythm, we will find God exalted more and our agenda, desires, and timelines exalted less.

INVITATION

Take five minutes and sit in silence. Go lock yourself
in the bathroom if you need to. Sit in the car a little
longer before your errand. Just sit, and be still. Know
that He is God.

Write down anything that may have come to mind
during that time.

Begin carving out time in your day to be still. Begin
setting a new rhythm for your soul to be still.

Abide

*F*ruit is the product of a much bigger process. It is what is revealed after a number of different things take place. It is an end result. The fruit is on the branch, which is on the vine, which is on the tree, which is in the ground. John 15 says, "Abide in me and I in you. As the branch cannot bear fruit by itself, unless it abides in the vine, neither can you, unless you abide in me." I cannot bear fruit unless I abide in Christ.

What does abiding look like though? A branch cannot bear fruit by itself. It must abide, or hold onto, the vine. The fruit is a result of the branch working with the vine. We cannot bear fruit in our own life unless we are with Christ. Fruit is what happens when we invite Christ in—when we sit with Him, walk with Him, be with Him. We cannot flourish or be fruitful unless we hold on to Christ. We must allow him to be a part of everything we do. I think of a money tree. Have you seen its trunk? It is actually multiple trunks that are intertwined, weaving around one another, and looking as if they are braided together. Abiding is God being intertwined in all we do—work, family, rest, play, worship. When we compartmentalize God from the rest of our lives, like church once a week, we are not abiding. When we invite God into our times of impatience, anger, bitterness, or lack of self-control, we allow his strength to take over rather than our own. We abide.

INVITATION

What areas of your life can you invite God into this week?

Take a minute to abide with God right now. Invite Him in. Ask Him to reveal where He wants to be more a part of your life.

Rest in the knowledge that fruit takes time to grow. With continued abiding you will see fruit.

Fruits of the Spirit

*T*he fruits of the Spirit are found in Galatians 5: love, joy, peace, patience, kindness, goodness, faithfulness, gentleness, and self-control. That is what I want. What I was ultimately praying for when I wanted to flourish. How do we get this fruit? I know for me I don't feel patient or kind. Self-control is a joke most days. I'd like to think I am a good person, and I know I am faithful. Love is always more complicated than I want it to be, and peace (oh peace!) I want so badly.

These fruits are exactly what they say they are—of the Spirit. When I start living in the Spirit, I will see fruit. But fruit takes time to grow. I never realized how much I try to do life on my own. Even when I told God I wanted to flourish, I thought it would be something I did on my own, hoping He'd shine His blessing down upon me as I went about figuring out my life. But I have to do life with Christ. With the Spirit. None of this I can do on my own. Bearing fruit. Pruning. Learning. None of it can be done alone. I must abide in Christ.

The Message Bible says,

> But what happens when we live God's way? He brings gifts into our lives, much the same way that fruit appears in an orchard—things like affection for others, exuberance about life, serenity. We develop a willingness to stick with things, a sense of compassion in the heart, and a conviction that a basic holiness permeates things and people. We find ourselves involved in loyal commitments, not needing to force our way in life, able to marshal and direct our energies

wisely … Since this is the kind of life we have chosen, the life of the Spirit, let us make sure that we do not just hold it as an idea in our heads or a sentiment in our hearts, but work out its implications in every detail of our lives. (Galatians 5:22–23, 25)

INVITATION

Write out which fruits of the Spirit that you feel you have.

Write out which ones you would like more of.

Tools

When I set out to prune our fruit tree, I quickly realized I needed the proper tools. Our loppers and rusty saw would only get me so far. I needed clean tools. I needed a ladder to get me higher into the tree. Each type of branch required a different type of tool. At one point I gave my son a quick rundown of where my phone was and how to call 911 if I were to fall out of the tree. I watched as my neighbors slowed their drive to watch the comedy of me high in a tree with loppers unfolded. That is when I knew I needed help, the help of someone stronger—another adult, like my husband.

We need more than just ourselves to prune away at our lives. We need different tools to help us combat impatience, laziness, insecurity, gossip, pride, lying, comparison. While some branches of life are easy to cut away, others require asking for more help— someone stronger, more stable, with more wisdom. A friend, a spouse, a parent, or even a counselor. We need accountability. We need someone who will point out the bad fruit in our lives. But we also need to be humble enough to reach out and ask for help. Counseling is a beautiful tool. That can be the big gun of pruning. Just like with our enormous cherry tree, which I cannot prune at all, there comes a point where a professional is the one for the job. There is no shame in that. It does not lessen our faith, but it is another tool the Lord has given to use in our lives.

Moses had both the accountability and wisdom of his father-in-law, Jethro. "Moses listened to the counsel of his father-in-law and did everything he said" (Exodus 18:24 Message). Jethro saw that Moses was taking on too much and would soon burn out. He encouraged him to seek out the help and wisdom from among the people. And Moses listened. He was trying to do it all on his own, but after listening to his father-in-law, "He chose capable men from all Israel and made them leaders of the people, officials over thousands, hundreds, fifties and tens" (v. 25 ASV).

INVITATION

Give all you are trying to do in life over to God. Lay it all out before Him.

What are you trying to do on your own that could use some help?

Who can you approach and ask for help? Ask God to bring someone to mind.

Would seeking the wisdom of a professional counselor be the wise next step for you? If so, I encourage you to make that phone call today.

Thorns

I remember the first time I ate a blackberry as a little girl. Some friends of ours had a small blackberry bush growing in their backyard in Ohio. It was the first time I had tasted fruit straight from nature. Picking the berry off of the vine and eating the plump, juicy fruit was an experience I have never forgotten.

Fast forward twenty-plus years and I am now living in a city that is almost overrun with blackberries. About an acre of our land, if left unattended, will be overtaken by blackberries. We let them go for a while once, and before we knew it they were taller than me. The best part about an acre of blackberries is the fruit itself. However, getting to wild blackberries can be a challenge. Their vines are filled with thorns, some small and unassuming, others large and frightening. I've learned to go in with long sleeves, gloves, jeans, boots, and loppers. Picking the perimeter is not so bad, but the farther in you get, the stronger the vines and the bigger the thorns. At one point we found loppers still clinging to a thick vine, a sign that a frustrated child had given up on his chore.

While working through a patch of blackberries and making my way farther into the tangled mess of vines, I couldn't help but think of how similar the blackberries and I are. I am a tangled mess. Sin has crept its way in, and past wounds have created a prickly shield. I still create good fruit, but much of the time it is hard for people to get to or even see. I can offer so much on the perimeter, but dig a bit deeper, and it's harder for me to let people in. I put up a shield. My thorns are my defense against getting hurt. People give up because I become too prickly. But thankfully there are others who get out their loppers and keep at it. They see past the thorns; they see the fruit that is there, sometimes buried deep. They keep with it. I try not to hurt anyone, but we all end up doing it, don't we? And I'm thankful for the grace and forgiveness of those who keep going. I am thankful for those who don't just abandon their loppers and walk away. Even though we put up shields, we desperately want to let people in, don't we? We need people who will keep at it with us. And if we have friends who do that, how much more does Christ do that? He gently cuts through our thorny vines. He keeps digging. He keeps inviting. He doesn't abandon us because we make it hard for him to enter in. Jesus has already endured the pain of the thorns for us.

So Pilate took Jesus and had him whipped. The soldiers, having braided a crown from thorns, set it on his head, threw a purple robe over him, and approached him with, "Hail, King of the Jews!" Then they greeted him with slaps in the face. Pilate went back out again and said to them, "I present him to you, but I want you to know that I do not find him guilty of any crime." Just then Jesus came out wearing the thorn crown and purple robe. (John 19:1–5 Message)

INVITATION

Thank Jesus for enduring the thorns for you.

In what ways do you put up your guard so as to not let people in?

Who can you allow in this week?

Throw Off

*H*ave you ever seen a tree or a plant that is not growing straight up and down? These plants have odd curves to them. If you are not sure what I am talking about, look up images of phototropism. Phototropism is the way a plant grows in response to light. It can either grow toward the light (positive phototropism) or away from the light (negative phototropism). While the negative response is very rare, a plant will do whatever it takes to receive light. It knows that in order to survive, it needs light.

When researching how and why to prune a fruit tree, one main reason that came up again and again was to allow room for light. It is necessary for light to make its way through the entire tree. Cutting back branches allows the healthy branches to grow toward and absorb the light. I, as the gardener, must help it shed these branches. You see where I am going with this? We must be pruned to allow light into our lives. We must cut away the branches that are blocking Christ's light from entering. In my own life I have branches—such as selfishness and mindless consumerism—that need to go in order to let the light of Christ in. Removing these things allows me to see what I should be growing toward.

So the pruning must take place. I must figure out what is keeping me from growing toward the light. Hebrews 12:1–2 says, "Therefore, since we are surrounded by such a great cloud of witnesses, let us throw off everything that hinders and the sin that so easily entangles. And let us run with perseverance the race marked out for us, fixing our eyes on Jesus, the pioneer and perfecter of faith." What do I need to throw off that so easily entangles? Just like there are many types of branches—suckers, whorls, crossing branches, and competing leaders—that can be pruned from a tree, there are many things—characteristics, sins, problems, idols—that need to be pruned out of my own life. Some may look innocent, such as mindlessly scrolling social media or staying up late, but they are sucking life away from the health of the tree God created me to be. And once I cut those back, I can run straight for Christ because I can see what I am running toward.

INVITATION

Do you feel as though it is difficult to see the light of Christ? If so, why?

What looks innocent in your life but might actually be sucking life away?

What is entangling you?

What can you throw off today?

Suckers

*G*ardeningknowhow.com tells me a sucker is "an odd branch that has started growing from the base or the roots of your tree. It may look much like the rest of the plant, but soon it becomes apparent that this strange branch is nothing at all like the tree you planted. The leaves may look different, it may produce inferior fruit or it may be a different kind of tree altogether." Why are these branches a problem? Suckers do exactly what the name suggests—they suck energy away from the main part of the plant. They grow so fast that they can soon overtake the tree. Gardentheraphy.ca tells us that "trees send up suckers as a reaction to stress. The tree is calling out for help." I must focus in on what causes those suckers.

What is the stress? I must ask God to reveal what my stressors are.

I asked my friends on Facebook what their suckers are. For some it's going to bed too late, following a "perfect" Instagram feed, or participating in social media's moral, ethical, and political debates. For others it is gossip at work, saying yes to too many things, mindless phone scrolling, or stressing over numbers (weight, paycheck, budget, etc).

I can relate to so many of these answers. It seems harmless when we are in the midst of it, right? *What's another Netflix show when I should go to sleep? This person will never know I'm talking about him or her. I must read the news to stay informed of the world.* These thoughts pass through our minds. We can justify our way through anything that seems harmless. Before we know it, we are not looking like the tree we were created to be. We are tired, unkind, discontent, and fearful. Our energy has been sucked away and given to things that don't deserve our attention.

We must carve out space to take a step back and

evaluate the health of our own tree. We must dig further and figure out what stressor might be causing us to allow these suckers into our life. When the weight of motherhood becomes too much, I tune out—I grab my phone and mindlessly scroll, escaping what I need to face. Perhaps not dealing with a loss in our lives has caused us to become bitter. Maybe a job has asked so much of us that we have disengaged with our families. When we name what is stressing us out and then take care of these things, those suckers will go away. When we ask for help in motherhood, face our hurts, or talk to our bosses, our need for mindless scrolling dissipates. Our bitterness will begin to melt away. Our desire to disengage lessens. And we begin to flourish.

INVITATION

Ask God what your potential stressors are.

How might those be the root of other areas you wish to cut back?

Ask God to replace the suckers with good fruit. (For example, bitterness with joy; escaping life with a desire to engage; fear with trust).

Overwhelm

Left to themselves, pecan trees will overbear. Too much fruit on the branch. So much so that even a breeze will crack the bow. Meaning you lose both the crop and the tree. Well, our lives are like those trees. We need to go through and pluck away those things in our lives that initially look beautiful but in the end just weigh us down. Whatever it is. We need to trim it away. And if we do our part, God will do his part by strengthening the bow. (*Finding Normal*)

But more fruit is good, isn't it? More people in our lives, more to-do's on our schedule, more food to eat, more toys to have, more clothes to choose from. It can all look so good. Like beautiful fruit on a tree. Like the pecans the pastor talked about in the movie *Finding Normal*. But we really know that if one more apple or pecan grows or if one more thing is put on our plates, we are going to break. But it looks good. So we keep adding, never cutting back. We want to appear as though we are flourishing, but really we are hurting. We are weighing ourselves down. We are going to snap. We don't want to say no. We're afraid of what people will think. We find our identity in all of the worldly fruit that we can show to people. We believe less fruit would mean we are less than. That is a lie Satan wants us to believe. He wants us to believe more equals better, more equals worth, and more equals success. But more is breaking us.

Here is the beautiful message: when we cut back the branches, the dead and the fruitful, God replaces them with more fruit. But not more fruit in the worldly sense, more fruit in the sense of what He knows we need and can handle. Pruning a branch makes it stronger when it grows back.

By getting into the mess of a tree that we are and cutting back branches, we begin to see what is really dead, what is rotten fruit, and what is good fruit. John 15:2 says, "He cuts off every branch in me that bears no fruit, while every branch that does bear fruit he prunes so that it will be even more fruitful." We can't let ourselves go, clinging to the lie that more is better. Sometimes more is really taking away from the healthy tree we are made to be.

INVITATION

What is a scenario when more is not necessarily better?

What fruit is hard to give up because it looks beautiful to other people?

What is weighing you down? Do you feel like it might cause you to break?

Give that over to God.

Choice

*T*here is a powerful story in the book of Joshua in which Joshua gathers all the tribes of Israel. After recounting all God had done for them since Abraham—reminding them how God had delivered them, handed enemies over to them, provided land they hadn't worked for—he tells the people of Israel to put away the god their fathers had served. He tells them to make a choice. Joshua tells them to choose who they will serve. Would it be the gods their fathers served or would it be the God who delivered them from Egypt? Joshua makes it very clear whom he has chosen to serve when he tells the Israelites in Joshua 24, "As for me and my house, we will serve the Lord."

The tribes go on to reply they would never "forsake the Lord to serve other gods."

There comes a point where we have to make a decision. We must choose whom or what we want to serve. Will it be the gods around us? Will it be God himself? We must filter our decisions through the sieve of whom or what we are choosing to serve. If we choose to serve the world, success, money, and power become our objective. If we choose to serve God, humility, generosity, and service become our fruits.

INVITATION

Write down who or what you choose to serve.

Start each day this week by making a declaration to serve God.

Comparison

When I led the mom's group at church, I had each of the women bring in an object that represented something they were good at. Pinterest had peaked, and women were feeling the effects. We were comparing our lives to the "Pinterest perfect" image and feeling not good enough. So we were giving up all together. Not even trying. If it couldn't be perfect, then we were swinging far the other way and claiming imperfection as part of the role of a "real mom." But I wanted them to see themselves differently. I wanted them to see each other differently. We each took our turn sharing our objects. Some shared with confidence while others shared with hesitation. One woman brought in a planner because she helps her husband keep the business books. One brought in a spatula because she is a great baker. Another brought in glue because she loves to craft. And a few women didn't bring anything. They couldn't think of one thing they were good at. Not one thing. This is a lie—a lie Satan wants us to believe and claim for ourselves.

You are gifted. You have talents. You are made to be a part of the body of Christ. Yes, we shouldn't think of ourselves as better than we are, but to do the opposite is just as offensive. For some, their giftings are obvious. For others, they may take years to uncover. Sometimes we want to be good at something when we are not; sometimes our talents seem meager or less glamorous than another person's. It can be dangerous when we start looking around and comparing our giftings, or seeming lack thereof, to others.

The pear tree that sits next to the cherry tree in our little orchard does not wish to be a cherry tree. Even though the cherry tree is larger and seems to be queen of the orchard, it simply relies on God (and me) to care for it, to prune its branches, to keep it in good soil, and to keep it well watered. And it produces fruit. It does exactly what it was made to do. And the same with the cherry tree. Some people prefer pears while others prefer cherries. Pears are wonderful to can or to make into sauce while cherries are an amazing snack or delicious in a pie. They each serve different purposes and different people. We are not made to be like everyone else.

"So since we find ourselves fashioned into all these excellently formed and marvelously functioning parts in Christ's body, let's just go ahead and be what we were made to be, without enviously or pridefully comparing ourselves with each other, or trying to be something we aren't" (Romans 12:3–8 Message).

Your gift of listening is needed for a hurting friend, even if it's not sexy. Your gift of leading a church of fifty people in worship is needed for a small community, even if it's not shared on social media. Your gift of cleaning the soup kitchen at the end of the day is needed for those who don't have a place to lay their heads at night. These are your gifts. And that is exactly what they are, gifts. They are what you give to other people. Your ear, your shoulder, your baked goods, your encouragement, your wisdom, your laughter. Denying who we were made to be or shoving it down because we think it isn't good enough is a disservice to those around you and to the kingdom of God.

This world needs you to share your gifts, to be exactly who you are and no one else. What an honor it is to use our gifts for the glory of God. When we shift our focus from how the world sees our gifts to how God sees us, it doesn't matter what attention we get or don't get. By using our gifts, we become the living, breathing expression of God on the earth, and that is beautiful.

INVITATION

What are your giftings?

What ways do you love to use your gifts?

How can you use your gifts this week?

If you are not sure, ask a friend or family member what he or she sees as your gifts.

Ask God in what ways he wants you to shine for His glory.

Seasons

"The grass withers and the flowers fall, but the word of our God endures forever" (Isaiah 40:8 NIV). The word of our God endures forever. I love that. No matter what the season, the Lord will still stand. He does not waiver when the winds blow. He does not hide away when the rains come. He is not good to us only when the sun shines. Even though the seasons of life change, this does not mean the Lord does. I want to say that again. Even though the seasons of life change, the Lord does not change. "Jesus Christ is the same yesterday, today and forever" (Hebrews 13:8). This is truth. This is the truth we need to hold on to when everything else in our life is telling us that God is not there. That God has abandoned us. That God has moved on to someone else. I feel like the father in the book of Mark who asked Jesus if he could heal his possessed boy. Jesus heals the boy, and the father exclaims, "I do believe! Help me overcome my unbelief." I believe God never changes. I believe He is the same yesterday, today, and tomorrow. But, boy, do I need help overcoming my unbelief. Even after seeing miracles take place.

There is a scene in the documentary *Won't You Be My Neighbor* where Daniel Tiger is asking Lady Aberlin if he is a mistake. Trying to comfort Daniel Tiger, Lady Aberlin tells him he is not a mistake, he is just fine, he is her friend, and he is loved. They go on to sing a duet together. Daniel Tiger is singing his questions of doubt while Lady Aberlin is singing her words of comfort.

It is not easy to quiet doubts. But we can make them a duet. We can sing our doubts to God while he also sings to us His words of truth and comfort. They don't scare God. Our doubts. Our questions. Our fears. He already knows them. Silencing them does not hide them from God. We can question God's whereabouts when we are in a season of darkness. We can question God's goodness in seasons of hopelessness. But we must be bold and confess those doubts. Confess those fears. Confess unbelief. It may not make them go away, but it will open us up to hear the duet of love that God is singing alongside of us.

INVITATION

What do you doubt right now?

Is it hard for you to admit these to God?

Share with Him your doubts. It's okay; he can handle it.

Ask God to show Himself to you today.

Roots

But Blessed is the man who trusts in the Lord, whose confidence is in Him. They will be like a tree planted by the water that sends out its roots by the stream. It does not fear when heat comes; its leaves are always green. It has no worries in a year of drought and never fails to bear fruit. (Jeremiah 17:7–8 NIV)

*R*oots serve three main purposes for a tree: they serve as an anchor, holding the tree in place; they absorb water and nutrients from the soil; and they store food. In his book *Rooted*, Banning Liebsher says, "Significantly, in order for a plant to survive, much less bear fruit, its root system has to take up more space underground than the plant takes above ground." There is an entire underground system in place to keep a tree healthy and solidly in the ground. Before it ever sprouts from the earth, its roots are being developed. And when that tree is fully mature, anchored by its healthy roots, it can withstand anything.

I think of a friend who was just diagnosed with breast cancer. I picture her standing on a Midwest porch, seeing the dark clouds in the distance, knowing she will have to face the storm head-on. It is time for her strong roots to do their work. She must trust that Father God will hold her firm. Her roots were grown before the storm ever developed. In her days of calm, before the diagnosis, she took in the water and nutrients of the Word. It was in the mundane, day-to-day of life that she stored her food, preparing for anything that could come her way. Her roots were grown while investing in community and deep relationships—people who will lend her strength in the days to come. And when the winds of cancer whip around her, I know she will stand firm.

Do we ever stop to consider what we are rooted in? Do we ask ourselves if we are anchored well? Most of the times we don't realize the health of our roots until a storm comes. Are our roots clinging to financial security or a particular relationship? Or are they nourished by the Word of God, community, and healthy habits? When we plant ourselves in the Lord's perfect love for us, we will not fear when the storms come (1 John 4:18).

INVITATION

What are you rooted in?

How can you strengthen your roots today?

Has there been a time where you felt you were not well rooted? What could you have done differently?

When was there a time that God held you firm in a storm?

Soil

*I*n the parable of the sower in the book of Matthew, Jesus tells his followers that where a seed lands—rocky soil, dry ground, among the thorns, or good soil—affects whether the seed is able to grow.

The health of our soil will determine the health of our tree. Our soil can be our friends, coworkers, social media influences, books, news stories, family members, and so on. If we aren't the flourishing tree we wish to be, could it be because our soil isn't healthy? What are we surrounding ourselves with? Is it the thorns of pride or envy? Is it the rocky soil of gossip? Is it the dry ground of unhealthy relationships?

Fruit will not grow if the base of the tree is not cared for. Are we watering the soil of bitterness by not forgiving? Are we watering the soil of addiction by not admitting our struggles? Are we watering the soil of fear by not turning off the news? Or are we watering the soil of gratitude by praising God in all circumstances? Are we watering the soil of generosity by sharing what we have been given? Are we watering the soil of love by caring for ourselves and for others?

We reap what we sow just like we grow what we water. "It had been planted in good, well-watered soil, and it put out branches and bore fruit, and became a noble vine." (Ezekiel 17:8 Message). And what do you know to be true about the growing of a seed? It takes time. We must plant the seeds of the tree we wish to be, water it with the abundance of Christ, and watch it produce branches and leafy boughs. We must not give up. We must persevere.

> What a person plants, he will harvest. The person who plants selfishness, ignoring the needs of others—ignoring God!—harvests a crop of weeds. All he'll

have to show for his life is weeds! But the one who plants in response to God, letting God's Spirit do the growth work in him, harvests a crop of real life, eternal life. So let's not allow ourselves to get fatigued doing good. At the right time we will harvest a good crop if we don't give up, or quit. (Galatians 6:8–9)

INVITATION

Read over the questions again posed above. Do you relate? Are there other areas in which you are watering healthy soil? Unhealthy soil?

What can you stop watering today?

What have you planted that you are patiently waiting to see grow?

Harvest

*D*id you know that God will do more than we can ever ask or imagine? I believe this, but I don't live like I believe this. Can I say it again? I love *The Message* version of Ephesians 3:20: "God can do anything, you know—far more than you could ever imagine or guess or request in your wildest dreams." My dream was to flourish. God will do more than allow me to flourish. I must ask. I did ask. He took me to places I didn't expect. He asked of me things I didn't know I needed to do. It has been a difficult journey learning the ugliness of my ways and learning what needed to be cut away. But cutting those things away has allowed light to come in. It has left more room for Christ. My energy can now go toward nourishing the good fruit. I am learning to plant the seeds of what I want to see in my life. I am learning to be patient in the watering. I am learning that I will harvest what I sow. I am learning to trust and live out what Matthew 13:8 says: "Some seeds fell on good earth, and produced a harvest beyond his wildest dreams."

INVITATION

When you think of a harvest, what picture comes to mind?

What do you want to be harvested in your life?

Do you believe God can do more with that than you could ever imagine?

Flourish

"May the golden notes of autumn remind us that everything we lost, every falling thing, serves to enrich and deepen the very soil our life grows in."—Nicollete Sower

Some people choose a word for themselves each year. A word to focus on and work toward. In asking God to flourish, I realized I had chosen a word for myself. As each new year has approached and my yearning for a new word beckons, it is difficult for me to choose another word. I don't feel as though I have accomplished my previous year's word. I don't feel as though I can move on past "flourish." I want to look back over the year and say,

"I have flourished. Check. What new word should I conquer this year?" But I have learned that flourish isn't something I arrive at. I can't check it off of a list. If I have learned anything through studying the fruit trees, it is that to flourish is an ongoing process. When I look out over our little orchard throughout the year, the trees look different from season to season. Whether there is fruit on the tree or not, I know they are alive. Whether their branches are filled with apple blossoms or there are brown leaves clinging to the last of fall, I know the trees are healthy. They are going through the life cycle a tree goes through. Flourishing is a constant cycle of death, new leaves, flowers, fruit, and repeat. It will be like this throughout my entire life. Just like the seasons: times to cut more branches, times when I am abundant with good fruit, and other times where it only seems as if I am bare with nothing to show for my life. I will always be pruning. I will always be checking in on my health. I will always have to abide with Christ—take in His living water and be rooted in Him. I can't help but think of John 10:10: "I have come that they may have life, and have it to the full." Christ gives us a full life; He enables us to flourish. This is why He came.

INVITATION

Do you choose a word for yourself each year? If so, have you thought about asking God what word he would have for you?

Invite God into the process of hearing and living out that word.

Ask God to show you how you are flourishing.

In what ways is your life full today?

Invitation to the thirsty

"Come, all you who are thirsty,
come to the waters;
and you who have no money,
come, buy and eat!
Come, buy wine and milk
without money and without cost.

"Why spend money on what is not bread,
and your labor on what does not satisfy?
Listen, listen to me, and eat what is good,
and you will delight in the richest of fare.

"Give ear and come to me;
listen, that you may live.

I will make an everlasting covenant with you,
my faithful love promised to David.

"See, I have made him a witness to the peoples,
a ruler and commander of the peoples.

Surely you will summon nations you know not,
and nations you do not know will come running to you,
because of the Lord your God,
the Holy One of Israel,
for he has endowed you with splendor."

Seek the Lord while he may be found;
call on him while he is near.

Let the wicked forsake their ways
and the unrighteous their thoughts.
Let them turn to the Lord, and he will have mercy
on them,
and to our God, for he will freely pardon.

"For my thoughts are not your thoughts,

neither are your ways my ways,"

declares the Lord.

"As the heavens are higher than the earth,

so are my ways higher than your ways

and my thoughts than your thoughts.

"As the rain and the snow

come down from heaven,

and do not return to it

without watering the earth

and making it bud and flourish,

so that it yields seed for the sower and bread for the

eater,

so is my word that goes out from my mouth:

It will not return to me empty,

but will accomplish what I desire

and achieve the purpose for which I sent it.

"You will go out in joy

and be led forth in peace;

the mountains and hills

will burst into song before you,

and all the trees of the field

will clap their hands.

"Instead of the thornbush will grow the juniper,

and instead of briers the myrtle will grow.

This will be for the Lord's renown,

for an everlasting sign,

that will endure forever." (Isaiah 55 NIV)

Acknowledgments

I wish I knew each person's name who contributed in some way to this book. For everyone at WestBow Press, thank you for believing in this project.

To Sam. For being a listening ear. For never doubting. For creating space to allow these words to form. For your grace. Thank you.

To Soren and Eva. For cheering me on. For your questions. For your trust in me. Thank you.

To my family. For raising me. For supporting me. Thank you.

To Mica. For your edits. For your wisdom. For your understanding. For your patience. Thank you.

To Juvy. For your direction. For your guidance. For your encouragement. Thank you.

To my girls, you know who you are. For your Marco Polos. For Your Voxers. For your coffee dates. For your long walks. Thank you.

Printed in the United States
By Bookmasters